# TWO BY TWO

## FAVORITE BIBLE STORIES
### BY
### HARRY ARATEN

**KAR-BEN COPIES, INC.**     **ROCKVILLE, MD**

*for my mother*
*- of blessed memory -*
*and my father*
*and their grandchildren:*
*Devra, Yaël, Gideon,*
*David and Jeffrey*
*—H.A.*

Library of Congress Cataloging—in-Publication Data

Araten, Harry.
    Two by Two: Favorite Bible Stories / Harry Araten.
        p.    cm.
    Summary: Presents popular stories from the Old Testament, in simple text and illustrations.
    ISBN 0-929371-53-4
    1. Bible. O.T.—Biography—Juvenile literature. 2. Bible stories, English—O.T.—Juvenile literature. [1. Bible stories—O.T.] I. Title.
    BS551.2.A68   1991
221.9'22—dc20                                                                                    90-46841
                                                                                                      CIP
                                                                                                       AC

Published by KAR-BEN COPIES, INC., Rockville, MD 1-800-4-KARBEN
Printed in the United States of America

# CONTENTS

# ADAM AND EVE

After God created the heaven and the earth, the trees and the flowers, the birds and the animals, God created man. God called him Adam, from the Hebrew word for earth, *adamah.*

God put Adam in the most beautiful part of earth, the Garden of Eden, where good things to eat grew on wonderful trees. In the very middle of Eden was a special tree, The Tree of Knowledge of Good and Evil. Adam was told to take care of the garden and to eat from all the trees, except from the Tree of Knowledge. God saw that Adam was lonely, and made a woman to be his partner. Adam called her Eve, which means life.

Now the serpent in Eden walked and talked like a person. But he was evil. He urged Eve to eat from the forbidden tree. "You'll be almost as smart as God," he promised her. So Eve ate the fruit and gave Adam a taste.

Adam and Eve were ashamed that they had disobeyed God. They tried to hide, but God found them and punished them. The serpent was forced to crawl on his belly forever. And Adam and Eve had to leave the Garden of Eden.

# NOAH AND THE ARK

The children and grandchildren of Adam and Eve fought with each other. God grew angry that the people who were created to care for the world were destroying it. Only one man, Noah, taught his sons to be good and to listen to God.

God told Noah to build a giant boat called an ark. It was to be three stories high, and very long and wide, with many rooms of different sizes. God would bring floods to cover the whole world and drown out all the wickedness. But Noah and his family would be saved, along with two of every living thing. This was God's promise to Noah.

When the ark was finished, Noah took his whole family and two of each animal, bird, and insect into the ark, with enough food for all. Heavy rains began to fall. Big waves appeared in the oceans. For forty days and forty nights, the waters grew higher and higher. And the only ones left in the whole world were those safe in the ark.

# AFTER THE FLOOD

The waters drowned all living things except those safe in the ark.

God remembered the promise to Noah. After 150 days, the waters started to go down, and the ark came to rest on the very top of Mount Ararat, in the country now called Armenia. Noah opened a window and sent out a big, black raven, who flew round and round as the waters dried up. Then he sent forth a white dove, but the dove could find no place to land.

The following week, Noah sent the dove out again. This time, the bird came back, and in her mouth, was a leaf from an olive tree. Noah waited one more week, and this time the bird left and did not return. Noah knew that the dove had found a place to land. The earth was dry, and it was safe to leave the ark.

God blessed Noah and promised never to flood the earth again. As a sign of this promise, a rainbow appeared in the sky. To this very day, anyone who sees a rainbow remembers God's promise to Noah.

# ABRAHAM AND SARAH

Abram lived about 300 years after Noah. He and his wife Sarai were happy together, even though they had no children. One day, God told Abram that he and Sarai should leave their homeland and travel to another country, where they would become founders of a large family. Abram and Sarai trusted God, so they packed up their household, and made a long journey to the land of Canaan.

"This land will be for your family, who will be as many as the stars in the sky," God promised them. As a sign, God changed their names to Abraham (father of many nations) and Sarah (princess).

Years passed, but Abraham and Sarah still had no children. One day, Abraham was sitting in his tent, when three strangers passed by. He hurried to greet them, and to offer them food and rest. One guest announced that by the following year, Sarah would have a baby. Sarah laughed, thinking she was too old, but sure enough, a year later she gave birth to a boy. Abraham and Sarah named him Isaac, which means laughter.

# ISAAC AND REBECCA

When Isaac grew up, Abraham decided that his son should marry. He sent a servant back to his birthplace to find a wife for Isaac. The servant arrived outside the city near the water well.

"When the women come to draw the water," he thought, "I will ask them for a drink. Let one of them also offer my camels a drink. By her kindness I will know she is the one chosen to be Isaac's wife."

Just then, Rebecca, Abraham's niece, came to the well and began to fill her jar. The servant asked for a sip of water. "Drink," she said, "and I will also bring water for your camels."

When the camels had finished drinking, Rebecca invited the servant home. He asked permission to take Rebecca back to Canaan. Rebecca and her family agreed. When Isaac and Rebecca met, they loved one another and were married.

# JACOB'S LADDER

Isaac and Rebecca had twin sons, Jacob and Esau. They were very different and did not get along. Jacob tricked his father into giving him the blessing meant for Esau, who was the first-born son. Esau was angry that Jacob would become leader of the family, and vowed to punish Jacob. Jacob ran away.

When it grew dark, he stopped to rest. He took a big stone for a pillow and lay down on the ground. Jacob slept and dreamed. He saw a ladder reaching from the earth all the way to heaven. Angels were going up and down the ladder. Then Jacob heard the voice of God. God repeated the promise made to Jacob's grandfather Abraham, that the land he was sleeping on, and the land all around as far as he could see, would be for Jacob's family and their families, forever and ever. Jacob called the place of his dream Beth El, the House of God.

# JOSEPH AND HIS BROTHERS

Jacob gave his favorite son Joseph a coat of many beautiful colors. This made Joseph's brothers jealous. One day out in the fields, they captured him and sold him to traders, who brought him to Egypt. Joseph became a servant to the king, who was called Pharaoh.

Now Joseph was smart and could explain people's dreams. Once Pharaoh had a dream about seven fat cows and seven thin cows. Joseph told him this meant in seven years, Egypt, the land of plenty, would become a land of hunger. Joseph told Pharaoh to store food for the future. Pharaoh agreed, and put Joseph in charge of the fields and distribution of the food.

When the famine struck, Joseph's brothers came to Egypt in search of food. Joseph forgave them for selling him into slavery. He sent them home to bring their father Jacob, and the family settled with Joseph in Egypt.

# MOSES

A new Pharaoh who came to rule Egypt did not remember Joseph and all he had done for the Egyptians. This Pharaoh made the children of Israel slaves, and ordered that all newborn baby boys be drowned.

One couple, Amram and Yocheved, hid their baby for three months, until his cries became too loud. Then Yocheved made a floating basket out of river grass and placed the baby in it. She put the basket on the edge of the river. The baby's sister, Miriam, hid in the tall grasses to see what would happen to her brother.

Pharaoh's daughter came down to the river to bathe. She saw the basket floating by and asked a servant to fetch it. When she saw the baby crying, she picked him up and comforted him. She decided to keep the child and called him Moses, which means "taken from the water."

Miriam asked the princess if she needed a nurse to help with the baby. The princess agreed. Miriam told her mother, and so it happened that Yocheved was able to care for her own son and teach him about his people.

# THE TEN COMMANDMENTS

Moses grew up to become the leader of the Children of Israel. It took many miracles, but he finally convinced Pharaoh to let them leave Egypt. During the day, a large cloud led them, and at night, a magical fire pointed them in the direction of the Promised Land. When they came to the Sea of Reeds, also called The Red Sea, the waters parted and the Israelites crossed to the other side.

When they arrived at Mt. Sinai, Moses climbed to the very top. For forty days and forty nights he was on the mountain. God gave Moses two tablets of stone, engraved with the Ten Commandments. These were rules teaching people to care about each other and to respect their friends and neighbors. God told Moses to teach these rules to the people of the world. We follow them to this very day.

# RUTH AND NAOMI

When a famine came to Bet Lechem, Elimelech and Naomi moved to Moab with their sons. Soon after the sons married, they died, as did their father Elimelech. Naomi decided to return to Bet Lechem. Her Moabite daughter-in-law, Ruth, begged to go along.

"Wherever you go I will go," she said. "Your people will be my people, and your God will be my God."

Ruth and Naomi arrived in Bet Lechem at the time of the barley harvest. They were hungry and tired, so Ruth went out to gather leftover grain in the field of Boaz. Boaz heard of Ruth's kindness to Naomi, and told his harvesters to let many stalks fall in Ruth's path.

After a time, Boaz and Ruth married. She gave birth to a son, Oved, who became the grandfather of King David.

# DAVID AND GOLIATH

The Philistine army invaded Israel and set up camp high on a mountain. King Saul gathered Israel's army on an opposing mountain. In the valley between, the giant Goliath, the Philistine's best fighter, dared King Saul to send his best man to fight him.

David, a young shepherd, heard Goliath's threat. He knew that God protected him from wild beasts in the field, and would protect him from Goliath, also.

David wore no armor and carried no sword. He took a sling, put five smooth stones in his pouch, and walked into the valley. Goliath laughed when he saw the young boy. "You have shining armor and a big sword," David said. "But I come in the name of God."

Goliath rushed toward David, waving his sword. David took a stone from his pouch, put it in his sling, and spun it over his head. The stone hit Goliath between the eyes, and the giant fell to the earth.

David would grow up to be Israel's greatest king.

# JONAH

Jonah was a prophet who taught the people God's word. One day, God told Jonah to leave Israel and go to the city of Nineveh, to warn the people of their evil ways. Jonah didn't want to save the people of Nineveh, so he boarded a ship to Tarshish, hoping that God might forget about him there.

Soon after the ship set sail, a storm raged, and the sailors were afraid the ship would sink. They decided that someone on the ship was unlucky. Jonah confessed that he was running from God, and the storm was his fault. He ordered the sailors to throw him overboard. Immediately the strong winds stopped, and the waters became quiet again.

God sent a giant fish to swallow up Jonah. For three days and nights he prayed to God and promised to do what he was told. The fish opened his mouth, and Jonah came out on dry land. God told Jonah once again to go to Nineveh, and this time Jonah went. He told everyone that God would give them 40 days to change their wicked ways, or the city would be destroyed. The people listened to Jonah, and Nineveh was saved.

# ESTHER

In the land of Persia lived the rich and foolish King Ahasuerus. When his queen, Vashti, refused to appear at his royal banquet, he banished her, and held a contest to choose a new queen.

A Jewish man named Mordechai, brought his young cousin Esther to the palace. She won the king's heart and was crowned queen.

Haman, the king's evil prime minister, was angry that Mordechai would not bow down to him. He plotted to destroy Mordechai, and all the Jews in the kingdom. Haman cast lots *(purim)* to determine the day on which the Jews would die.

When Mordechai heard that his people were in danger, he begged his cousin Queen Esther to appeal to the king. For three days she fasted and gathered her courage. When she approached the king, he was happy to see her. She invited him to bring Haman to a banquet. While they were eating, she revealed Haman's evil plot. The king became angry and ordered that Haman be killed. The Jews, happy to be saved, celebrated with great feasts, gifts to the poor, and merrymaking. This holiday, which we still celebrate today, is called Purim.

# DANIEL

When Nebuchadnezzar, King of Babylonia, captured the holy city of Jerusalem, he burned down the Temple and forced the children of Israel to leave their country. The king ordered his officers to bring the smartest of the young Israelites to his palace in Babylonia. One of them, Daniel, was chosen as the king's personal servant. When Darius took over the kingdom, Daniel stayed on to be the new ruler's trusted helper.

The king's officers were jealous of Daniel, so they persuaded Darius to pass a law forcing people to pray only to the king. Anyone who disobeyed would be killed. Then they told the king that Daniel prayed to the God of Israel.

Darius had no choice but to punish Daniel. He put him into a cave of wild lions, and covered the opening with a big stone. When Darius came to the cave the next morning, Daniel was unharmed. The lions sat around him quietly, licking his hands. Darius, impressed by the power of Daniel's God, ordered the children of Israel back to their land to rebuild the Temple in Jerusalem.

Harry Araten was born in Casablanca, Morocco in 1936, and studied in New York City. For more than 25 years, he has had one-man international art exhibitions. He and his wife Rachel, and children Devra, Yaël, and Gideon, currently live in Israel. His first book, *Angels & Others,* was published in 1989.